RV

Also by Bob Miller

An Angel Named Zabar

*Toto Coelo: By the Whole Extent
of the Heavens*

RV

Bob Miller – Nan Kilar

RV

Published by Wheatmark™
610 East Delano Street, Suite 104
Tucson, Arizona 85705 U.S.A.
www.wheatmark.com

International Standard Book Number:
978-1-58736-819-6
Library of Congress Control Number:
2007923915

FOOL AM I

"They said, 'You simply must visit the vineyards in France and taste the grapes.' And so I went, saw and tasted. The vineyards were well kept, the grapes tasted like grapes, and the people were pleasant. Then I found, by chance, a vineyard that was more pleasing to my eye, a grape that embraced my palate, and people who were more than pleasant; they were like family. And I didn't even need a passport; all this was in my very own country." —Bob Miller

CONTENTS

INTRODUCTION

Love to travel? Thinking about buying a recreational vehicle? We've been there and done that, and thought we'd share the experience with you in hopes of saving you the unnecessary stress and costs we endured. Bottom line, go for it; but do so with your eyes wide open to the fact that you are the prey, not the predator. There are two kinds of RV deals: 1) You buy what you want. 2) You buy what someone wants to sell you.

I truly enjoy traveling in our RV. But in all honesty, if I could afford to fly first class, stay in five-star resorts and take guided limousine tours, I wouldn't bother with an RV. Simply put, I don't look forward to the daily chores, especially the black water (potty) tank duties. And before my Significant Other, Nan, would touch the dump hose, she'd be in enough protective gear to make her over-dressed to work at a bird flu laboratory.

Buying a used RV makes cents. Why? Buying a new RV is not a good business decision unless you're absolutely certain you can use it as a tax write-off. Buy a new RV and you've lost thirty cents (30¢) of every dollar invested by the time you've traveled ten miles in your now used RV. You will drop another ten percent the following year. Now add that loss to the cost of using the RV, divide that by the miles driven, and Enron stock would look pretty good.

An RV, like your child's braces, is not a money-making investment; but the rewards can be beautiful. Imagine pulling off the road in your RV and watching elk during the mating season. It's an experience I'll never forget. The females, whatever they're called in the elk world, are unbelievably like human females. This poor guy was trying to keep his gals away from a big male on the other side of the road. No sooner would he usher one back on his side of the road when another would try to sneak over to tall, dark and handsome patiently waiting on the other side. I'm sure he was the older (and wiser?) of the two. The point of this story is that a tour bus had pulled over to watch this. All the passengers crowded over to one side assuring that no one got to enjoy this event. Keeping to his schedule, the bus driver pulled away after just a few minutes while we watched this National Geographic scene over a second pot of coffee.

CHAPTER ONE

WHAT TO BUY?

You can buy an A, B or C class, a fifth wheel (we haven't run into anyone yet who has a good explanation for that term) or a travel trailer. Or you can do as real campers do who are up to the challenges of pitching a tent and fending off critters both big and small and save your kids' inheritance.

Class A motor homes are self-contained with many amenities. Most have at least one slide-out; many have three or four slide-outs. In our opinion, one is better than none. All of them come with a shower, commode, microwave, fridge and TV; many also have a washer/dryer, automatic leveling jacks and plush interiors with wet bars. Some are gas; some are diesel pushers (the diesel engine is in the back so you're not bothered by the noise and smell). The average lengths range from about 28' to 45'. Add all the toys you want, but know that along with the initial cost comes the continual upkeep cost. In the event that cost is not a consideration, Nan and I are available to do your RV shopping for you. We'll even put the first 10,000 miles on it just to make sure that everything is in good working order.

Class C motor homes are on a van chassis with overcab bed/storage space. Most are fully self-contained like a class A, but only the longer ones have a walk-around bed. Actually, that term is misleading. At best it's a tight squeeze; but in Nan's opinion, a tight squeeze is better than no squeeze at all. The pilot and co-pilot seats are just van seats, not nearly as comfortable as the big captains' chairs in a class A. But if your trips are short (500 miles or less), a class C could be for you. If you are considering a C in hopes of saving money, you're in for a surprise. I've owned both and money is not a good reason to buy a C over an A. Two good reasons might be that the C is usually shorter and, therefore, easier to store, and the engine is more accessible.

Class Bs are just big vans with the rear seats removed and some amenities put in their place. You might like showering in the middle of your 'kitchen'; we don't. Obviously, you'll get a little better gas mileage with a B. The big advantage, as I see it is easier handling, and it's much easier to find mechanics to work on it simply because it will fit in their shops. To some extent, a class C owner enjoys this benefit too. Nan and I just couldn't see putting all that money in a vehicle that would end up parked in front of a motel room half the time. Again, it's all about one's lifestyle that's important. A Class B owner informed me the last time out that they were very pleased with their choice in a recreational vehicle. He explained their goal was to get from point A to B with as few stops as possible, while having the option of pulling into a rest area or park for the night if they desired. He went on to say that while he and his wife enjoyed the onboard potty and refrigerator, they couldn't see hauling around a queen size bed, two night stands and a chest of drawers. These people, like Nan and I, are happy because we bought what we wanted, not what someone wanted to sell us.

Fifth-wheels are towed by your pickup truck (possibly a diesel truck). They can be quite long and luxurious and have plenty of headroom. However, it's really quite challenging to walk back to get a Coke or use the bathroom while traveling down the road. It might be worth mentioning that in most states, if not all, it's against the law to ride in the back while the fifth-wheel is being towed. Nan just reminded me that the fifth-wheel runs really quiet and she'll bet money that it gets better gas mileage than our Class A. I never really gave the late George Burns the credit he deserved until I met Nan. "Say good night, Gracie."

A travel trailer is the granddaddy of all the above and offers the same advantages and disadvantages as the fifth-wheel. There are some towing advantages to the fifth-wheel, or so I'm told; but having never owned one, I'll not tout one over the other. I do know that the price of the travel trailer is usually much less than the fifth-wheel, and that fact alone should speak volumes. My suggestion to those who can't decide between buying a fifth-wheel or travel trailer is to talk to those who own a fifth-wheel or travel trailer. I don't think motor home owners, as a group, would be a reliable source.

Chapter Two

WHERE TO BUY?

J like any vehicle, you can buy a new or used RV from a dealer. If it's a used RV, you have the option of buying from an individual as well. That's your decision to make....who do you trust?

Answer: No one. Not even yourself. Most purchases, even pricey ones, are made by emotional decisions instead of logical ones. So what's the solution? Research begets knowledge. Make a list, check it twice, and don't leave home without it.

An individual will proudly tell you all about his/her RV and, of course, will most likely tell you only about the good stuff. If you choose to buy from the individual, you may be better able to negotiate the price and conditions of the sale. The big advantage buying from an individual is the hands-on instruction for driving, setting up and tearing down that particular RV. Be sure to ask for all manuals and maintenance records.

Buying from a dealer. If you go into an RV dealership with the idea you're going to be disappointed or cheated, you'll leave with your expectations met. But, it'll not be the dealer's fault; it'll be yours.

Do the dealer and yourself a big favor. Go there with the list of your wants and needs that you've checked twice. Have the answers ready for questions like:

How much do you want to spend? Will you need financing? Will the RV be used by two or a large family? Do you plan on towing a vehicle? Do you want leveling jacks? Want a satellite television tracking system? One, two or more slide outs? What floor plan do you want? Want a king size bed, walk-in closets, split bath?

You can get prices for all of the above and more amenities online. And learn the pros and cons of these things before you buy instead of after you buy.

Eureka! You think you've found the RV of your dreams. Now what? Check the RV carefully inside and out and decide for yourself if the coach is really what you're looking for.

What about a pre-buy inspection? Good idea and good luck. Unbelievable as it might sound, most consignment dealers will not allow you or your mechanic to thoroughly inspect the vehicle. They claim that since the vehicle is not theirs, they're not authorized to allow such inspections. Naturally, they are authorized to allow their mechanics to do a pre-buy inspection for you for a fee. And under no circumstances would I recommend buying an extended warranty from a dealer. They are simply selling some other company's warranty and passing the cost on to you in addition to another fee for handling the paperwork. Even though I purchased an extended warranty, I'm not sure I would do it again. It's a crap shoot either way.

CHAPTER THREE

RV EQUIPMENT

Big and Little Items
And Tips for Use and Maintenance

You might want to bookmark RV service websites. One thing to take into consideration is that your RV, unlike your home, could be in Florida sunshine in the morning and freezing rain in Georgia that evening. In short, if you want your coach and the installed equipment to serve you, then you'd better keep them serviced.

I can't speak for other owners, but since our coach is out of warranty, I do a limited amount of preventive maintenance like changing the oil and filter. I mean, it's just a Chevy 454 Workhorse, and with sixteen inch tires, I can easily slide under it when we're lucky enough to stop at a park with paved sites. That makes it inexpensive and provides me with peace of mind knowing the pan plug and filter are not leaking. Plus, I don't like to go over 2,000 miles between oil changes. I take it to a professional service center about every third time so they can lubricate it as well.

Airbags: No, not the ones in the dash or side panels. These are the airbags that are inside the front axle springs. Like your tires, the air pressure in these bags should be checked regularly. That's the easy part. Determining the correct pressure based on your RV's configuration might require you to search through the manufacturer's manuals. And that's not all bad; I'm forever saying things like "Wow! I didn't know that." Just for the record, I keep 60 psi in the bags on our 31' coach.

Note: In the event the air bags on your coach need replacing, my suggestion would be to have them replaced at Camping World. If that's not practical, order them and let a front-end mechanic in your area install them. However, should you decide to do it yourself, here's how the mechanic who installed the new ones on our coach did it: He used a vacuum and sucked all the air out of the new ones. Then used cable ties to make a neat little bundle, slid them in and then cut the ties. Brand to buy? He suggested Air Lift, and that's the ones we went with.

Air Conditioner: Those who have never tripped a circuit breaker in their RV when turning on an appliance can't appreciate the improvements made in the last few years by RV manufacturers and their component suppliers. Coleman-Mach is one of those companies. Their Mach 3 P.S., in our opinion, is one of the best air conditioners you can buy, especially for those of us on a 30 amp system. And before I forget it, I personally wouldn't buy an RV that had a heat pump unless it was connected to a 50 amp system. Back to the Mach 3 P.S.--it's an air conditioner designed to use less power without sacrificing cooling performance. So you can stay cool and run your other electrical appliances and toys. In order to save you a big shock in the event you buy a used coach and discover on a hot day that your air conditioner is low on Freon, you'll soon be hearing from the service manager that they do NOT recharge these roof air conditioners. Adios $500.

Furnace: We prefer a small electric heater to running the big furnace at night. It's not about saving the gas. The little heater keeps the RV very comfortable in 30-degree weather, and we feel much safer. Hey, we're paying for the electricity, so why use our gas? One of Nan's favorite sayings is, "I save where I can to spend where I want to." Regardless of the time used, the furnace, like all the other gas appliances in the coach, should only be serviced by qualified people. I'll do without one of these appliances before I'll mess with it beyond cleaning as recommended by the manufacturer until I can get it fixed.

Furniture: What should you do with unused or seldom used pieces like a chair? We took ours out and haven't missed it at all. The little extra room it gave us is wonderful. On nearly every trip we meet owners who have had their dinette taken out and replaced it with table and chairs. Not us, we really like the solid attached dinette and, besides, it makes into a bed. We'll never use the bed, but if we decided to sell our coach, it might be a selling plus.

A comment about getting the carpet and furniture steamed cleaned. You can rent one of the little steam cleaners at most grocery stores, but I would advise against it for two reasons. 1) They seldom, if ever, clean and disinfect these machines. 2) The little machines are not powerful enough to get out the dirt unless you pre-spot and soak the material. If you're not really careful, you could end up with a much worse problem than dirty carpet and stained furniture—mildew. Most professional carpet cleaners today have powerful truck-mounted steam cleaners that will get out most of the water and cleaning solution. We found that nearly every one of thcm had a different price, so shop around.

Generator: We rarely use the generator, but are glad to have it. We keep it serviced so it's in good working order when we do need it.

This is all I know about our generator. The brand name is Onan. If there's another brand being used in RVs, I don't know about it. It has never failed to start and supply all the power we've needed, but I'll give Nan and myself some of the credit. We never overload it. They tell me that you can adjust your battery charge rate at the inverter/charger. Wonderful--what is it and where is it? No, don't answer that question. I don't want to know. I'm afraid of electricity. Nan and I will just use only those appliances needed when using the generator. We live in Florida, and Mother Nature has trained us well in the art of getting by with no power. I do know if you have to charge up your batteries, regardless of the generator being used, it takes time. No matter what brand generator you end up with in you coach, go to Onan's website. There's far more information about these AC/DC critters than you'll ever need at: http://www.onan.com/onan/index.jsp

Hand-Held Two-Way Radios: We paid only $19 for a set of walkie talkies. The specs, according to the instructions in Spanish, Japanese, French and German, stated there were 38 privacy codes and had about a 6-mile range. They're so handy and a comfort to have. We use them if one of us is in the car and one in the coach (Bob has been known to drive off with the hood open). They're also really handy when we're parked and one of us is inside and the other is outside. Shoot...I've wished we'd had them in Target so I could find him!

Ladder: You'll most likely need a ladder for your RV. If you have a ladder on the back, naturally it'll get you onto the roof; but if you need one to reach a high point in the front of the coach, it's a lot of work to get the one on the back off. Don't get carried away like I almost did and buy one of those big extension ladders. Any five-foot-two honey, like Nan, can easily clean the windshield and do other chores with a three-step ladder, but they won't. A three-step ladder is much easier to store in one of your compartments. For those of you who can spend $300, you can get a Telesteps telescoping extension ladder. They're fun to play with. Extends up to 10 ½ ' and down to 28 ½ " in seconds, automatically. Telestep claims that the ladder meets OSHA and ANSI standards. All I got to say is that these two, whoever they are, have higher standards than Nan and I.

Propane and the Tank: We try to keep ours three-quarters to full because not all parks sell propane. Never, and I mean never, use a wrench on the fittings, and keep oily rags far away from the tank. A good rule, and one I adhere to faithfully, is to touch nothing and do nothing in that compartment with the exception of opening and closing the on/off valve. And here's a big tip: open it very slowly. I've been told most tanks come with a shut-off mechanism that shuts the system down if it detects a leak, and opening the on/off valve too fast can fool the sensor. I don't know if that's true or not, but I open that valve slowly. Oh, and before I forget--if after you finally get the on/off valve all the way open and none of your gas appliances work, check the little leak detector switch that is most likely located down at the floor near the kitchen range. If it's turned off, the system is shut down.

This leak detector switch is a very finicky

little devil. If you spray any chemicals like mosquito spray and the alarm starts shrieking, your gas system is shut down. Now you must wait for the air to clear and then reset the switch before you'll be back in business. I decided to mosquito proof the entire coach our second night out and emptied a can inside. I said smiling, "Mr. Mosquito, just try and get me now." Off in the distance I'll swear I heard, "No problem. You're coming out here." About that time the gas detector went off and out I went.

Since we stay at full hook-up sites, we need the propane only to keep the fridge running while driving. We turn the water heater on only while parked and we're awake; last one to go to bed turns off the water heater, first one up turns it on. There's still enough warm water for washing hands throughout the night. Yes, the stove needs propane, but I do my best to talk Nan out of cooking, so we seldom use it. I guess it was our first full week together that Nan made pancakes for breakfast. When she asked me how I liked them, I said something to the effect that they were a little too hot for my taste. She replied, "I thought I might have used too much cayenne."

Rear Axle Sway: I'm talking about the one when you're driving, not parked for the night. The former can be unnerving. Passing semis and strong crosswinds can cause the RV to swerve a bit, so keep an eye out for approaching trucks. Known as "the tail wagging the dog," rear axle shift causes the front end to steer itself. I cannot guarantee it because I have not yet had this product installed, but I've been told the Supersteer Rear Stabilizer Bar will help correct this problem. Out-of- pocket cost for the product and installation is about $500 at Camping World. (800-626-5944 or campingworld.com.)

As side note, I would suggest you order a Camping World catalog even if you're still in the looking stage. You'll have a better idea of what you're getting into with an RV, and the list of Camping World locations around the country is great to have when you're on the road.

Refrigerator: All I can say is it takes awhile for the darn thing to go from hot to cold. The exact opposite of my first wife, but Nan says it's entirely possibly that I was to blame for that.

The Fridge Fan is a small, handy device to reduce the initial cool-down in your refrigerator. Just put two D-cell batteries in when you start out on your trip and place it on the bottom shelf of the refrigerator; take the batteries out when you store the coach. It's $15 well spent.

We make it a point when putting the RV in storage, even for a few days, to empty the refrigerator, clean it, and leave the door propped open a few inches. When taking the RV out of an outside storage facility, I suggest you remove the refrigerator vent cover on the outside of the coach to make sure no creatures have made it their home. These propane/electric refrigerators are expensive, so take care of it. There are those who suggest you turn the refrigerator off while moving for safety reasons.

Note: If you need some reason to spend $600-$800--just operate your RV refrigerator without leveling the RV. It'll take a few times of doing this before you'll achieve your goal, but you'll get there. I might add that if you smell ammonia, and you're not wearing one of those expensive French colognes, you're just about ready to say, "Honey, I did it. You're going to get that new refrigerator."

Here's a website that you might add to your favorites. Again, one of the very best sources of information about buying, selling and traveling in an RV, is the Internet. http://www.cdtrv.com/rvtrouble. htm

Roof: The odds are that you have a rubber roof. And in my opinion, that's a good thing. Now, just because it's out of sight for the most part, you can do yourself a big favor and keep it in mind. This part of your RV takes an awful beating from the elements. I suggest you clean it with warm, soapy water. After it dries, sponge mop a UV treatment on. It'll only take about an hour to clean and treat. Besides keeping your coach dry, you'll enjoy the bonus of eliminating the vast majority of little unwanted white streaks (chalking) on the outside of your coach. It takes only a half gallon to treat our 31' RV, about $15 per treatment, and 30 minutes of our time. We use *Protect All Rubber Roof Treatment*.

FYI: It's not actually a rubber roof. The scientific name for it is Ethylene Propylene Diene Monomer, or EPDM for short. It was initially introduced to the Recreational Vehicle industry in the 1980's as a cost cutting shortcut. It's one of those cost-cutting moves by the motor home industry that turned out to be a real plus for everyone concerned. Visit the *Protect All* website (http://www.protectall.com/) and get the low down about that thing on top of your RV.

Shocks: So you didn't check the shocks or the tires, and now the guy who's putting your new tires on points out a shock that's broken off and gives you the bad news that all the shocks are worn out? That's not surprising since manufacturers usually go with the standard equipment. And in no way are shocks on a van chassis that was designed to support six passengers up to the task of dealing with a two bedroom apartment. In this case, there's two words you should remember: Bilstein shocks. The chances that your tire dealer will have these shocks in stock are very slim. They're high end equipment. What to do? My suggestion would be to go to the nearest Camping World and get the shocks put on. If they are too far away, you can order the shocks from them or directly from the manufacturer and have them installed locally.

I've had a couple of bad experiences at Camping World; but to their credit, they've tried to correct the situation. Again, the only way you'll get the full benefits from an RV, new or used, is to get involved. Learn how it works and how to keep it working.

Note: I'm not into NASCAR, but I do listen to what the top mechanics in NASCAR have to say about equipment, and they say a lot of nice things about Bilstein Shocks.

Storage: Most recreational vehicles come with ample storage, but you have to be a bit more organized in an RV. You'll need to put some thought into what goes where. You can do it the hard way as Nan and I did to start with. We simply put stuff wherever it would fit. That was fine until we needed that item. Then she'd start at the back and I in the front opening doors and pulling out drawers until we found the thing we needed.

A good example of storage is the bed in our RV. There is no box spring. The mattress simply rests on a plywood board that can be raised up revealing a large storage area. The mattress and plywood board are held up by two cylinders, one on each side for easy access.

This is one of those stories where you had to be there to appreciate it. I was in the process of putting a new battery in my hearing aid, and just as I put the thing back in my ear, came this loud banging on the door. I opened it and the guy who owned the coach parked next to ours, asked if there was a problem and could he be of help? I stood there confused. Then came this screech from the bedroom. "You old, deaf moron, get your butt back here!" While vacuuming under the mattress, Nan had tripped over the cord and fell in. I guess the contraption thought she was through and closed.

Tires: In the event your pre-buy inspection falls short and you get stuck with some bad tires, in most cases this will be dry rot since the vast majority of RVs spend more time in storage than on the road. Here's a product you should consider: Michelin tires (http://www. michelinrvtires.com/). This brand is not your only choice, but it's a darn good one. You should budget at least $450 per tire. In most cases, this will get new tires put on and balanced. Do NOT buy into the BS that the sand bags that some truckers use are as good as the spin balance and weights (front tires). You can have automatic air pressure sensors installed that will keep you informed of the tire pressure as you make your way across this magnificent country of ours for about $600; or you can do as peasants like me do and check the pressure each morning before pulling out (always check tires when they are cold).

Please, even if you don't care for Michelin tires, go online and watch their video about how to handle a blow-out. It's short, free, and works for all types of vehicles, not just RVs. It's a life saving few minutes. You might also look into having either Safe T-Plus or Steer Safe installed. In the event of a blow-out, these devices work hard at keeping your front tires going in a straight line, giving you time to get back in control. Quiz: If you have a blow-out, do you step on the brakes or gas? If you're not absolutely sure, watch the Michelin video.

TV--Satellite vs Antenna: Don't have a satellite on our coach, so I can't offer any advice based on experience. I suppose if I had the bucks, I'd go with Winegard's RoadTrip SDi in-motion set-up ($2,100 unit only). My second choice would be the DirectTV plan. It'll not keep the kids entertained while on the road, but it'll only cost you about $50 a month. I think they throw in the little antenna. Most parks now offer cable, and some have the cost built into their nightly rates. In the event you're a bit more fugal than I am, you can use the batwing antenna. We have one, but the only thing I've been able to get on it was an old bat.

Valve Core Extenders: Talk about a Catch-22. They're a wonderful time and finger saver when they don't leak. If you never use it, a valve core wrench is still worth having in your tool kit. In my case, it's not really a kit. Nan was having trouble opening a drawer and said "it's yours" if you can open it. Hey, now I have a drawer all my own. That brings up a suggestion. If you're not a knowledgeable automotive mechanic, don't load your RV down with tools you may never need. If you're like me, you'll unfix more things than you'll fix. Honestly, I don't know what else there is to say about valve core extenders. Where I buy tires there's a guy who says he could talk all day about them. If you're interested in that sort of a thing, I can set up a meeting.

Vent Covers: We put air vent covers on all three of our vents. But if I had to do it over, I'd only install a cover on the living room vent that has the Comfort Air fan. Reason being, this little fan does a super job of keeping the air circulating in the coach, thus helping to control dampness when the air conditioner is not running.

Here's a little tip about turning the bathroom fan on. Don't. At least not for the purpose you use it at your other home, odor. I'm not saying that yours stinks, it's just that the RV commode sits over a holding tank. And that fan, small as it is, pulls whatever odor there might be in that tank right up into your coach. Spend a few dollars and buy two Cyclone vents. They replace the two standard roof pipe covers, and by design, cause the odors in your grey and black water tanks to be sucked out by the slightest breeze. This can be very entertaining while driving the coach down a two lane road. After the air flow sucks the odor out of the tanks, it travels back over the coach and down into the windows and vents of the vehicles behind you.

CHAPTER FOUR

DRIVING AN RV

If you've never driven an RV (or big truck) before, you're in for a real treat—just remember this is NOT a car! A motor home accelerates more slowly than a car; brakes on a gas RV react differently than on a car. At first the RV will seem wider than the lane marked on the road, but eventually you'll get used to the fact that you do fit within the lane. One of the hardest things for Nan and I to get used to was staying close to the center line. We invariably allowed the coach to drift too far right. That's where the bridges, trees, and other dangerous objects are that don't cut you any slack and move out of your way. Ever since I hit one of those plastic orange construction barrels, Nan introduces me as Mr. Magoo.

You have only two giant side view mirrors and no rearview mirror. On really cold days you might, as we did, need a way to defog the side front windows so you can use your side view mirrors. If there is no defroster vent that blows on these windows, you can coat them with a defog product. Rain-X makes a good one and you can get it at Wal-Mart. I mention this here in hopes you'll address the problem before pulling on to a busy interstate as I did. It's the little mistakes, mistakes you can get away with in a car, that'll get you into big trouble driving an RV.

We try to stay in the right lane as much as possible. On interstates though, you have to watch out for the merging vehicles since many drivers don't know that merge means to step on the accelerator. You have two choices when this happens--slow down or just keep going and let the mergers decide to speed up or slow down. I've done it both ways and the latter, even if the other driver makes the right decision, could return to you in a nightmare with a totally different ending as it did me.

Weight can drag your RV down. Keep heavy bottles, canned food, and liquids to a minimum. Good weight distribution is very important as well. If it's not absolutely needed, leave it at home. Why haul 100 gallons of fresh water 300 miles to your next stop when fifty gallons would be more than enough? On the other hand, extra fuel is not an unnecessary weight to haul around, at least not in my opinion.

Speaking of weight, I've read several articles that suggest you have your RV weighed. They gave some good reasons for doing so, but I've not taken the time to do it. I reason that since we do not load our RV down with stuff, and try to balance the coach evenly with the stuff we do bring onboard, it's not necessary. Being a retired pilot I know that these are NOT good reasons for skipping this duty and obligation. Here's some worthwhile information from *RV Safety & Education Foundation, Inc.* **(http://www.rvsafety. org/index.htm)** that I hope you'll use. Please visit their website.

You must have a good knowledge of your personal weight-carrying requirements. A few helpful figures; (pounds per gallon)

- Water: 8.3
- Gasoline: 5.6

- Diesel Fuel: 6.8
- Propane: 4.2

As you calculate your requirements, keep in mind that EVERYTHING you put in the RV has weight. The average couple carries approximately 2,000 pounds of "stuff", while the average full-time RVers carry an average of 3,000 pounds.

I recommend Michelin tires and not Goodyear tires simply because I don't remember ever buying Goodyear and know nothing about their product. But since I'm sure there are thousands who have, I'd like to offer their loyal customers their advice on the importance of getting your RV weighed and their website (http://www.goodyear.com/rv/weighing/).

Your RV must be weighed when it is fully loaded. This includes passengers, food, clothing, water, fuel, supplies, any towed vehicles, and the tow vehicle for a fifth wheel or travel trailer. It is important to weigh your RV at a location that can provide axle-end specific weights. You should not expect to measure equal loads at both ends of the same axle because floor plans and component locations vary significantly; however, you should distribute the load to obtain the best balance possible.

Some places where you can weigh your RV:

- RVSEF Weight & Tire Safety Program - a service offered at many RV rallies and shows
- CAT Scales
- Weber Son & Service Repair Inc.
- Truck stops
- Farm co-ops or feed mills
- Some sand and gravel yards

Use the following guideline to ensure proper tire inflation pressure for motor homes and RV trailer tow vehicles: Determine the heaviest end of each axle and use that load to select the inflation pressure for all tires on that axle.

CHAPTER FIVE

PLANNING YOUR TRIP

It's not a good idea to jump into an RV and take off like you'd jump into your car to run to the grocery store. I didn't say that I hadn't, I just said it's not a good idea. Putting some thought into the route you're going to take to Yellowstone, Big Bend or grandmas will save you money and reduce road stress. A good hardcopy road atlas and GPS work well together. Turtle Central is a website with links to campgrounds and map grids for the respective cities. Go to http://www.bob-millerwrites.com/. More on RV parks in a later chapter.

We installed Co-Pilot 10 (http://www.alk.com/) on our laptop to use in the RV. Driving from point A to point B on an interstate isn't rocket science and the GPS program isn't needed. But going from point A to point B via red roads or wanting to catch certain points of interest along the way is when the GPS is really useful. The co-pilot (a/k/a Significant

Other) can watch your progress on the screen, and the program gives verbal info at intervals you have pre-programmed. It also allows you to select routes that avoid propane-restricted tunnels and low clearance bridges. It's truly a handy tool to have on the road.

Another consideration in your planning is whether you're going to tow a car or use rental cars. We have chosen to rent when needed and haven't been inconvenienced by that decision. We just didn't want to pull the extra weight in the mountains, not to mention getting even less gas mileage than our current 8 mpg. The few times we've needed to rent haven't been prohibitively expensive, so we've stuck with that plan. If you choose not to tow, just keep in mind that you can't run to the grocery store (or anywhere else) on the spur of the moment. So you must carefully plan your grocery stop to a) get everything for the next few days and b) get the groceries at a store with a big parking lot.

What vehicles can you tow behind an RV? 1. A four-wheel drive vehicle. 2. A vehicle with a drive shaft that can be disconnected. 3. A car that allows a transmission lubrication kit to be installed. The Saturn is the car that most reports favor and is the hands down winner with RVers year after year. Go on line and you'll find dozens of reports and recommendations.

CHAPTER SIX

RV PARKS AND CLUBS

If your RV is self-contained, of course you can stay anywhere within reason. We prefer to hook up at an RV park...the nicer, the better in Nan's opinion. Finding a nice park isn't as easy as it sounds. As mentioned in an earlier chapter, we've spent a lot of time checking websites hoping to find really nice parks on or near our intended route.

Of course, some websites look just great and when you actually get there you wonder where the pictures were taken since the park is not truly as advertised. But most RV parks are pretty friendly and fellow campers can answer a question you may have or offer you a sack of fruit from her grapefruit tree.

We personally don't care for RV parks that are heavily treed. The narrow roads within the park, trees to dodge getting in and out your spot, and squirrels playing on your roof are bad enough. But trees are dangerous weapons if a storm comes through...you don't need a tree or even just a limb falling on your RV or flying through one of your windows.

Amenities are varied, so read any park info carefully to be sure you're getting what you want. We prefer pull-through sites with full hook-up (water, electric, sewer). However, you may be very happy with a back-in site or partial hook-up (water, electric). Cable TV, laundry, playground, pool, tennis courts, game room, etc. are just a few of many other amenities you may or may not want or find at an RV park. Like us, you might also be interested in where the wireless hot spots are when advertised at a park. We've considered getting an antenna to extend the range of the wireless card built into our laptop.

There are several camping clubs you can join for a nominal annual fee that entitle you to discounts at certain RV parks. You'll find these parks in the respective directory of each RV club you join. Other benefits of joining these clubs include a mail forwarding service and insurance on your RV...definitely the best deal we found. RV windshields are big and expensive, so I suggest you make sure your insurance company provides no-deductible glass coverage.

FYI--We ended up with a cracked windshield and were delighted to learn that our GMAC policy had us covered and there was no deductible. We bought the insurance through Good Sam's Club at a sizeable discount. It was some 35% less than we had been quoted by the company we have our cars insured with. Having said that, I strongly advise you join all RV clubs for the very minimum time offered. You can always renew your membership.

CHAPTER SEVEN

SETTING UP AT AN RV PARK

I get out and go into the office to pay for our stay and get the map showing what space we'll call home for the next night or two or more. Then Bob slowly drives to that site trying to follow my directions while not running into the oldsters zipping around in golf carts oblivious to all activity around them.

Bob pulls into the spot and I try my best to guide him, if necessary, to get as close as reasonable to the sewer, electric box and water faucet. Then he gets out the leveling blocks, places them where necessary and directs me while I try to nudge the behemoth forward or backwards 'til it coach is level. As level as possible is good so doors open and close properly, you don't have to walk up or down hill when inside, and your tank sensors read properly.

We work together to get set up for our stay. First, we hook up our hose to the city water faucet at the site (hoping their faucet is in good working order and we don't get an unexpected shower) and fill the fresh water tank, if necessary. Then we screw the hose into our water filter for the duration of our stay. Next plug in the RV's power cord to the electric box (get it in the right amperage socket), and connect our TV cable if it's offered at the site. Don't forget to close your utility compartment door (you did remember to run the cables and hose through the opening in the bottom of the compartment, didn't you?).

Bob doesn't hook up to the sewer hose 'til the next morning when he empties the gray and black water tanks.

WHILE IN A PARK

If you don't do a lot of grilling at home, the chances are you'll not do a lot on the road. Therefore, I suggest you take a few trips before you buy a lot of grilling equipment and propane canisters.

We found what we use and enjoy the most is a little $9.95 1.5-quart crock pot. Plan your grocery list to include a chuck roast and veggies, put them in the pot, plug it in, go hiking or sightseeing and when you return, Wow! The enticing smell fills the RV!

Unless you live in a rural area, you probably can't store your RV in your driveway. So some tasks must be done in a park while on the road. My beloved promised me grand scenery, lots of fun and exercise in our RV. OK...I can handle that easily. However, his idea of exercise was polishing the behemoth; definitely not my idea of exercise, even though my biceps increased in size. And scaling great heights is not climbing a ladder in my opinion. But ain't love grand?

CHAPTER EIGHT

LEAVING AN RV PARK

OK. You've had your fun in the mountains or at the shore and it's time to leave this nice RV park and move on to your next stop. Time to unhook, unplug, and turn off.

While I'm waking up or eating breakfast, Bob checks the battery water level, checks the tire and airbag pressures and cleans the windshield (he does all that even if we've stopped for just one night).

Then we (or Bob) empty the black and gray water tanks. See the Sanitation chapter about those lovely details. Assuming I've got everything done inside that needs to be done (I usually run the vacuum cleaner every morning), the electric and TV cables are unplugged and coiled up in the utility compartment. The water is the last to be disconnected and we drain and coil up the hose. The utility compartment is sprayed with Lysol and closed.

I get behind the wheel and Bob directs me off the leveling blocks and stows them. I get out and we both check to be sure all compartment doors are shut, the batwing antenna is down if the park didn't have cable, the hood is closed and the steps are in. With everything inside secured for travel, we're off!

CHAPTER NINE

SANITATION

I don't know what the coach manufacturer calls it, but I call it the utility compartment. Open that when you stop at a park to hook up all your utilities – water, sewer, electricity and cable TV, unless you have satellite TV or use your batwing antenna. Sure seems strange to hook up the city water so close to your sewer outlet, so we're VERY careful working in that area.

Neither of us likes bugs, and we certainly don't want any intestinal or tummy troubles. We're very particular about keeping the utility compartment clean and sanitary. First of all, we each have a pair of work gloves hanging on the side of the compartment. The water filter is installed on the wall of the compartment (rather than lying on the ground). We're very careful that the hose ends never touch the ground while connecting and disconnecting them, and while stored the ends are screwed together so no dirt or bugs can get in. After dumping the black and gray water tanks, we run water through the hose (while it's still connected to the dump) then spray the ends with Lysol. The sewer hose is stored in a hose carrier mounted on the rear bumper and away from the water hoses. Keep the compartment door closed at all times unless you want unwanted four-legged visitors who may fuss about leaving. Once everything is packed away to head off to our next destination, we spray the entire compartment with Lysol. The electric and TV cables also get sprayed since they've been on the ground.

We choose to spread ant and roach killer around the tires while the coach is stored as well as each night when we're parked.

Before starting out on a long trip, we run water into the commode and dump in about a half bottle of sensor cleaner. The other half bottle goes into the grey water tank. Upon arriving at our first stop, Bob empties the tanks (the stuff sloshes around during the drive). This ritual helps keep the level sensors in each tank clean so you get a true reading when you push the button on the control panel inside.

Two products to consider for cleaning the black water tank are the Flexible Swivel Stik or the Flexible Tank Wand...both are under $20 at Camping World.

A related comment about bugs: We keep all food such as cereal, crackers, cookies, coffee, etc. in Rubbermaid or Tupperware containers. The foods stay fresher and the containers keep the creepy-crawlies out.

A related comment about clean: We keep a large bottle of Purell handy at all times. Not only for a quick clean-up, but it's great to use on scratches or minor skin irritations. The high alcohol content kills germs and the hand cleaner cleans all body parts. No muss, no fuss, no smell.

A related comment about dampness/mold: Stay on guard and use safe products. You can get into some serious health problems because of mold and getting rid of it. Although it doesn't seem to bother

Nan, my system simply cannot deal with bleach; therefore, we do everything we can to avoid the moldy problem.

CHAPTER TEN

LAUNDRY

I thought my days of hitting the laundromat were long gone. Wrong! It's back to saving quarters and taking stuff to the campground laundry facility. Naturally, I haven't found one as clean as I would prefer, but that's life on the road and one inconvenience I can deal with. So about every three or four days, I head to the laundry as soon as we get parked while Bob gets the coach all hooked up. When I return, I go behind him to make sure he hasn't overlooked little things like packing dryer sheets around the utility lines and hoses where they leave the coach in the bottom of the utility compartment to discourage rodents from making our RV their home away from home. Don't know what it is about the dryer sheets that these critters hate, and don't care; I'm just glad they work.

I don't have (or want) an iron or ironing board in the RV so we obviously don't take clothes that will need ironing. I find that Weekender and Chico's Travelers line are ideal for RV life...both are washable (on the gentle cycle which most newer machines in laundromats have) and no ironing needed. But most of the time we're in jeans or shorts, and T-shirts so laundry is not a major problem. Of course, I keep Tide, Clorox and Shout in the RV; I pre-spot whatever needs it in the RV and then just take the Tide in the basket with the dirties to the laundry facility. I bring everything back in a clean bag and fold the stuff on the bed if the counters in the laundromats aren't too clean. I'm a little too fussy about stuff like that, or so Bob says.

What clothes to pack for your trip? Obviously, it depends on where you're going and how long you'll be gone. Two weeks in the mountains in June might mean warm clothes with a T-shirt or two if it should get warm. Away for two or three months traveling around the country and you have a challenge before leaving home. You'll need stuff for warm weather, cold weather, rainy weather, swimming, tennis, hiking, etc. Since we don't have two walk-in closets in our RV, we take a little of each and are sick of those clothes by the time we get home...if those clothes even make it home with us.

CHAPTER ELEVEN

LONG TERM STORAGE

We made ourselves a checklist so we'd be sure to remember all the nitty things to do when storing the RV and when taking it out of storage. Nan had the list on Word and every day for a week she'd update it with something else she thought of. The day she didn't touch the list, I knew it must finally be OK.

Putting the Coach INTO Storage:

Bob pulls the RV into our spot and gets out the leveling blocks; then I do my thing under his direction.

Inside the RV, we turn off the fridge and leave the doors open. Camping World's No Mold Refrigerator Door Holder is a handy device. This is a good time to remember to take the batteries out of the fridge fan. Turn off the water heater and turn off the propane. Of course, our handy little electric heater has been turned off and tucked away. We leave one vent open a little bit (it has a cover) so there's some air circulating. Then close the drapes on the front window and make sure all the blinds are closed. Last thing to do on the inside is turn off the main battery switches and lock up.

On the outside, Bob turns off the propane tank. Because we've stayed in a park the previous night, the black and gray tanks have been drained as well as the water hose. So we just walk around and check to be sure all the storage bins are closed and locked. One quick look up to be sure the TV antenna is down. Bob then spreads ant killer around all the tires of the coach and covers the exhaust pipes (with duct tape or a condom) so no critters or bugs make them their home.

We remove the cover from the car exhaust pipe and load up the car. We're soon home and within hours Bob is planning another RV adventure. Others (no name mentioned) have to unpack, do laundry, plow through the mail, etc etc.

Taking the Coach OUT OF Storage:

This procedure is pretty much the reverse of putting the RV into storage.

Remove the tape from the exhaust pipes. Unlock the door and turn on the two main battery switches. I get started on the inside stuff while Bob slowly turns on the propane tank. Via our handy radios, he lets me know when I can turn the propane on inside. While I'm turning on the water heater, the fridge and putting the batteries in the fridge fan, Bob is outside doing the 'guy' stuff. Check the tire pressure, check the airbag pressure, check the battery, check the washer fluid, remove fridge vent cover to check for nests, and charge the battery charger. See the Sanitation chapter about what we do to clean the tank sensors.

By this time, I have most or all of the stuff moved from the car to the RV and we're about ready to leave. Again, Bob guides me to move off the leveling blocks so he can grab them up and put them in their storage spot.

Leaving the car at the storage facility is a little easier than the RV. We just spread the ant killer around the car tires and cover the car exhaust pipe...for the same reasons we do that to the RV when storing it.

CHAPTER TWELVE

WINTERIZING

I suppose I could safely write around some published information about winterizing, but it would be foolish, not to mention, unnecessary. I can put you in touch with Mark Polk who can walk you through this chore. He's a super source for information that'll help keep you safe, happy, and better off financially than you might be otherwise.

Mark Polk runs RV Education 101 and its sister site, RV University, which are both excellent RV information sources. The only thing you need to do is type **Mark Polk RV** in a Yahoo search box, and off you go to RV school.

ABOUT THE AUTHORS

Nan Kilar: I'm originally from the frigid Midwest and recently moved to south Florida to be warm all year long. I was employed by Deere & Company for thirty years. Since I love to travel, everyone at work was interested in my stories when I returned from a hiking trip. Retiring gave me even more time to travel. For over four years, I've been doing editing for Bob's website. Retiring gave me more time to read, too, so I started writing book reviews for his site as well. My favorite genre is mysteries, and James Patterson is my favorite author. I usually hit Sam's as soon as one of his books comes out.

★

Bob Miller: Bob served as a pilot in Vietnam in 1969-70. He was awarded the Distinguished Flying Cross and the Air Medal. He challenged Richard Shelby for a seat in the U.S. Senate in 1992. He authored: *The Business of Assassination*, *An Angel Named Zabar*, *Taciturn*, *Toto Coelo*, *You Have My Word On It*, *The Newbe*. He produced the television show, *The Late Show*. Bob has traveled the world over as a golf instructor and golf ambassador and worked as the golf professional on Holland America's ms Westerdam.

Bob's books are sold through fine bookstores and online through Wheatmark. com, Amazon.com, Barnes & Noble.com, and Books-A-Million.com. Read book reviews by Nan Kilar and articles by Bob Miller at www.bobmillerwrites.com. Your comments are always welcome and can be sent to bwmiller@bellsouth.net.

Printed in the United States
73723LV00001B/13-105

9 781587 368196